The Secret Gardens
of the

Vieux Carré

The Secret Gardens
of the

Vieux Carré

The Historic French Quarter of New Orleans

Roy F. Guste, Jr.

Little, Brown and Company

Boston • New York • Toronto • London

For Mimi, as always

First Edition

Library of Congress Cataloging-in-Publication Data
Guste, Roy F.
    The secret gardens of the Vieux Carré /
Roy F. Guste, Jr. — 1st ed.
        p.   cm.
    ISBN 0-316-33224-0
    1. Gardens — Louisiana — New Orleans.
2. Gardens — Louisiana — New Orleans —
Pictorial works. 3. Vieux Carré (New Orleans,
La.) — Description and travel. 4. Vieux Carré
(New Orleans, La.) — Pictorial works. I. Title.
SB466.U65N7454   1992
712'.6'0976335 — dc20   92-3487

10 9 8 7 6 5 4 3 2

IMAGO

Designed by Mary Reilly

Published simultaneously in Canada by
Little, Brown & Company (Canada) Limited

Printed in Hong Kong

Acknowledgments

I offer my gratitude to all the people who assisted in the production of this work: Robert Abramson; Harold Applewhite; Alice and Lewis Barry; Mary Adele and John Baus; Lindy Boggs; Shirley and Eldred Cieutat; Ken Combs; Dan, mayor of Dumaine Street; Lynn Dicharry; Bill Fagaly; Stuart Gahn; Betty Guillard; Doc Hawley; Dale Leblanc; Rebecca Lentz; the Levecques; Brobson Lutz; Milton Melton; Betty Norris; John Ordoyne; Steve Scalia; Sharon Simons; Rodney and Frances Smith; Peachy and Henri Villère; Mary Louise White; Hal Williamson; the library staff of The Historic New Orleans Collection; and the many others who aided in the development of this work.

My special thanks to the horticulturalists and designers who assisted: Vaughn Banting, Steve Coenen, René Fransen, and Annie Zipkin.

Merci, mes amis.

Contents

Preface

The New Orleans French Quarter, or Vieux Carré, is a unique place for these United States. The French words literally translate to "old square." It is this old square that was the original city of New Orleans, drawn in Paris by the engineer de la Tour and physically laid out in its location on the east bank of the Mississippi by his assistant Adrien de Pauger in 1721.

The sprawling New Orleans of today has grown up around this central *coeur,* this "heart"; it beats to the rhythms of old cultures past and new peoples present.

The children of our forefathers were themselves unique: the Creoles, the descendants of the French and Spanish who settled this land and established this metropolis. And there were the children of the enslaved Africans, brought here to cultivate the sweet sugarcane. With a sprinkle of Germans here, a dash of Irish there, and a generous dollop of Italians to romance the pot, it is the children of all these people, separately and together, who make up the population of New Orleans today.

One aspect of the French Quarter that has not changed since its founding is that it is a living city — now a city within a city. Its residents are people who have chosen to either remain or to arrive of their own free will. It is a place where no one is trapped by circumstance. If the rest of New Orleans were to suddenly disappear, we would still have a complete community within our twelve-by-six-block grid: a small community, but complete nonetheless, and perhaps ideal. It is a diminutive city of neighbors. We of the Vieux Carré are accustomed to passing familiar faces at every turn. We are also accustomed to visitors, both from other areas of New Orleans and other cities of the world, who come to enjoy the quaint feeling of our *petite ville,* our little city.

Our streets still bear the names of the Bourbon-Orleans family: kings, regents, princes of France from the late seventeenth and early eighteenth centuries. Street markers remind us of old and temporary street name changes during the ensuing Spanish domination, before New Orleans was returned to France, to Napoleon, for transfer to the United States as its largest territory. We live engulfed by this history every hour of our days and nights.

We are keenly aware of the desire of others to know the secrets of our place. Daily, passersby peer into our courtyard entryways hoping to catch a glimpse of the life behind: the secret life that exists calmly and quietly in contrast to a bustling contemporary time. Ours is an expression of another age when life was enjoyed with a Latin fervor unknown in the rest of this country.

As a living community we are able to enjoy all aspects of our lives here. As a survivor, as a "real" place, not some bloodless developer's confection of a new "old place," the Vieux Carré stands testament to a people, to the Creoles and their compatriots, who perceive life as one that includes an ambience, a *tout ensemble,* a joie de vivre, in order to be complete.

The courtyards and patios of the Vieux Carré are living spaces. They are used and enjoyed, and rarely kept as pristine images of some designer's whim. The photographs will explain better than words the reality of these coveted and well-used spaces. Imperfections exist: as in all of life itself. But it is the degree of imperfection that warms and relaxes the heart in the acceptance of it. The patina of the French Quarter is here to be appreciated, not repaired. To continually restore this imperfect beauty would be to destroy its essence, and its essence is what makes it unique.

Enjoy, then, this glimpse as introduction to, or as remembrance of, an uncommon place: the Vieux Carré and its extraordinary secret gardens.

The Secret Gardens
of the

Vieux Carré

Introduction

My earliest memories of my lifelong interest and love for the secret gardens of the Vieux Carré begin rather indirectly as a result of time spent in the French Quarter during our marvelous Mardi Gras season in New Orleans.

As a child, and just old enough to be walking on my own, my parents would take me and my older sister to the French Quarter — the original city of New Orleans, which encompasses a six-by-twelve-block district — to our family's restaurant, Antoine's. We would climb the long stairs to upper rooms where we would meet with the throngs of other family members — great-grandparents, grandparents, parents, and the many children (all cousins) — to spend some lively moments of perennial reunion when familial ties, friendships, and camaraderie were reinforced.

Soft drinks for the children and cocktails for the adults would be enjoyed, along with varied appetizing tidbits prepared below us in the great kitchen on the ground floor, as we waited for the parades to begin. This yearly, citywide observance of the Carnival season would begin almost two weeks before the actual day of Mardi Gras, and the parades would roll nightly through the French Quarter, the Vieux Carré, or old square, of the city, riling the citizenry into a gradual frenzy that climaxed on Fat Tuesday, Mardi Gras Day. The celebration of that day itself derives from the Catholic observance of Easter Sunday, before which is the season of Lent. Lent is meant to be a time for penance and austerity — some forty days — during which time one gives up some pleasure (or food) in atonement for sins. Naturally, our forefathers the French, long before the founding of New Orleans in 1718, had celebrated the last day of freedom before Lent by a festival of overindulgence. The observance of the festival in New Orleans became par-amount to its Catholic residents and grew to fruition as a two-week-long revelry.

In those days, we, the children, would be the alarm for the coming parade. Out from the crowded upstairs dining room and onto the adjoining balcony that fronted the res-taurant on the second floor, overhanging the sidewalk to the street, we would march. There we would stand guard, perched, waiting and watching, with growing anticipation and excitement, for the first sign of the red flashing lights of the police cars that would precede the parade, clearing the width of the narrow Vieux Carré streets of the human jungle crowding the avenue. With the distant red flash of the first lights, we would fly squealing back into the inte-rior room with the clamored announcement, "The parade's coming, the parade's coming!" The adults, knowing that we had only seen the lights from a good distance, would take time to refresh their cocktails before they exited the cozy warmth of the interior for the chill of the exterior balcony.

On those nights in February or March (Mardi Gras is a movable feast), when the winds blew cold and strong through the streets, we would stand bundled yet freezing, uncomfortable yet excited, waiting for the first paraders to come into view. The truck with the flashing lights would pass first, to the din of the waiting throng on the streets below us. Next came six or eight exquisite stallions con-veying proud dukes dressed in all of their glorious Carnival majesty of lush velvets and satins, all masked and tossing the prized doubloons to lucky nearby onlookers. These are the coins that are minted individually for each parading organization, of which there are now some eighty, and thrown as souvenirs of the year's festivity.

Next would come the first float, a tall and magnificent

gliding papier-mâché tableau, almost high enough to reach us standing above the street, on which perched the king and queen of the parade, the proud agents of a sacred trust: to be Mardi Gras royalty. They would pass amid the cries of the throng; then would come a marching band playing the brassy rhythms of some popular song, cymbals crashing, bass drums pounding.

Accompanying all floats — and there would be some fifteen — would be an encirclement of brightly burning oil lamps atop a tall pole held by a carrier. These troupes of *flambeaux carriers* would encircle each float to illuminate the spectacle for the crowd. The carriers, who were simply referred to as *flambeaux,* dressed themselves in white sheeting from head to foot — which was blackened by the soot of the smoking lanterns — for protection against the flames they carried. They danced a rhythmic mambo to the beat of the brass bands as they cavorted alongside the tall, glittering rolling tableaux of bright colors and gold and silver foil leaf. These foils reflected the dazzling dancing flames. The masquers, riding atop their sparkling kingdoms, were appareled in glistening silk and satin costume finery of yellows, purples, reds, and greens and all colors that glimmered in the night. There the animated riders, smiling behind their guises of painted papier-mâché masks, played to the thrill of the crowd as they cast out their treasured token baubles in the form of sparkling beaded glass necklaces and myriads of trinkets of all variety.

On the street below us, the cries and shouts of "Throw me somethin', Mister!" from the throng to the paraders would precipitate a quick scrambling to the ground of treasure seekers, as the pinging sounds of a tossed handful of prized doubloons hitting the stone streets reached everhopeful ears.

Those nights were always cold. The crowd below hunched together for warmth and then lunged forward from the curb to get nearer to those in possession of such treasures as tossed necklaces, doubloons, and trinkets, tokens of the night's revelry.

As the cold wind bore down on the crowd in the streets, it stirred together the perfumes of the avenue with those of the street vendors confecting their sweet delicacies: the heady aroma of the pink cotton candy; the tobacco smoke of the crowd; the candy apples' sweetness, mingled with the fumes of burning oil from the *flambeaux* lanterns; the sweet incense of caramel corn; the fetor of the horses; the hot roasting peanuts; and the diesel exhaust of the tractors pulling their grand floats.

When the excitement of the parade was over, it would be time again to make our way through the narrow streets of the Quarter, back through what seemed like an endless number of blocks, to where the car had been secured for the time. It was then that the mysteries of the Vieux Carré came alive for me. Even though the excitement of the revelry was still ringing in my ears, my senses now turned to something even more exotic than a Mardi Gras parade.

As we made our way through the crowds, mingling and laughing and celebrating in the streets, our hands were held tightly, my sister and I between our mother and father for protection. Along these mysterious *rues* we voyaged, each of which called out some new mystery in a dark and wonderful way.

As we walked, I would catch a glimpse from time to time through the bars of a narrow wrought-iron gate between ancient buildings that stood then in a state of decaying beauty, as of some forgotten aged ladies, *les demimondes,* draped in faded and tattered finery from another era. Passing each iron entryway, I would steal another glance down a narrow side alley, or through an ornamental element set carefully into a battered wood door to provide the insider with a view of the outside. Through these doors I would be teased into imagining what was beyond. The faint light of the gas or kerosene lamps that glowed dimly from deep in the alleys and the secret places to which they led was the ultimate mystery, one shrouded in veiled beauty and secrecy. Beyond these buildings, back and hidden away from the streets, were the secret gardens of the Vieux Carré.

Those nights, when we returned home tired and excited from the evening's adventure, I would lie awake, those last moments before sleep, remembering not the parades and the frivolity but the mysteries of hidden places. Morpheus would soon descend and take me in his arms to dream enigmatic dreams of places yet unknown to me, of gardens filled with mystery and intrigue. Were there things as ghastly as the ghosts of the tortured slaves in the haunted house on Royal, or was there some diabolical voodoo ritual being practiced in that clandestine court behind the famed home of Marie Laveau, the long dead voodoo queen?

As the years progressed and I passed from adolescent to teenager, grade school to high school, my interest in the hidden gardens grew. On Saturdays, I would leave our uptown home and ride the streetcar down the line to Canal Street, which borders the north side of the French Quarter. On those days, my announced mission was a midday movie at one of the grand old downtown theaters where I would spend two hours quietly and safely secured. But after that, I would quickly sink into the Quarter and roam the streets, marveling at the beauty of the old streets and buildings.

The Quarter was not the fashionable place that it is today. No, it was a place that was run-down, decrepit, you might say; yet it had a beauty that could not be denied, like a fallen angel drifting softly in a timeless void where she could be observed but not possessed. And so, I observed.

From time to time, fortune would be with me and I would find a gate open or an old black mammy standing at the entryway of a hidden garden, swapping stories with the neighboring servants. She would catch me stealing a glimpse into the alleyway and say, "Come on, hon', git yosef' a look, but make it quick now, fo' ma' mistress fin's you back tha' goggling!" I would enter, quickly and quietly, relishing the excitement and the beauty about to be experienced in the court beyond.

The alley led past the side of the house to the courtyard. The ancient brick wall surrounding the court was inevitably covered with some flowering and perfumed vine, a honeysuckle or a Confederate jasmine. In the far corner there was a sweet olive tree, the brick surface beneath dusted with its fallen, yellowed perfumed blossoms. All around the base of the walls was a slightly raised planting section flush with giant elephant ears crowding out into the court under towering banana trees, whose huge lavender-and-fuchsia central blossom was birthing the first tiny fingers of the delicate banana fruit. A Japanese plum tree to another side would be heavy with fruit as was the ancient fig tree in a corner, so full of the largest, darkest purple fruit, as big as your fist, that the branches pulled wearily down to touch the very ground beneath.

A crescent-shaped, knee-high raised brick pond hugs the center of the far wall. The bricks are darkened in blotches with the slick green-black of a tight moss, while a fantasia of tiny ferns snuggles into the cool wet corners and cracks of the fountain pond.

A stream of water trickles delightfully into the pool, poured eternally by an elegant statue of a nude woman. Tempted beyond reason, I lean in, close to her bosom, to taste the cool waters flowing in a gentle stream from the urn in her arms. I am seduced. . . .

Fat goldfish hang close under the water's surface, beneath the veneer of protection conjured by the wide rounded leaves of the water lilies. Their tall blossoms stand upright in raiment of flushed pink, defying the necessary restraint of the life-giving waters below.

A movement to the side, a glimpse of motion out of the corner of my eye, a sinister reflection in the pond's mirrored surface; the fish dive deep into the murky depths for escape. A cat, black as a moonless night, encircles the garden on the crest of the walls and leaps high onto the roof of the neighboring house, seemingly taking flight as in its apparent weightlessness it floats up to the very heights of the roof's peak. I shudder slightly. The coolness of the yard is unnatural.

Regaining my calm, I am refreshed by the air's moist breath, air that is ever replenished by the greenery.

The fragrance of the flowers is overwhelming, an opiate to the addict. One fragrance fights against another to gain control of my senses. I surrender, relaxed, into this world of sublime serenity.

My reverie is broken by the call of the servant at the outside gate. I am dismissed to face the reality of life. Outside on the street, in the blazing afternoon sun, movement of the passersby is sluggish and heavy. I become as they, and make my way out of this dream place back to Canal Street, the streetcar, and home.

On entering my college years, I chose to live and work in the French Quarter, where I could drift deeper and deeper into my infatuation with its beauties. My first residence away from the family home was a small slave-quarter apartment overlooking an exquisite, lush courtyard. I felt very much at home in my worn and tiny brick building, on the second floor, with its narrow wood balcony overlooking the flora of the garden, the flora of an older and — in a decrepit way — more elegant New Orleans than the one I knew.

I spent my days studying at the university, my evenings at work in the restaurant, and my late afternoons and nights learning to love and enjoy my life and the world around me. In those early years I learned what it was to be in love, the pangs of being hurt, and what it meant to be alive.

My love for the gardens and courtyards increased and developed so that I soon measured the beauty of each new dwelling by the charm and complexity of the courtyard and its flora. From the simplicity of a balcony garden or a postage-stamp-size patio, planted with urns of night-blooming jasmine and honeysuckle, to the grand antiquated lush courtyard crowded in from the brick walls by the dense foliage of banana, elephant ear, ginger, and fern, I became a hopeless slave to their resplendence. How would I know that the enchantress of my life, my beguiling and possessive mistress, would be the Vieux Carré garden?

During the twenty-five years that I have now lived in the French Quarter, and in the many locations I have inhabited, I have spent countless hours in quiet thought and calm contemplation in the cool greenness of innumerable hidden courtyards. They are a part of my life — a warm and wonderful part of my life. My life is far better because of them, for I have given in to my passion and now record the charm, the allure, of the femme that has taken me as her victim — a willing victim, I assure you — for all the curious to know.

I will venture forth now to bring you those secrets that live in a world apart, beyond the plastered walls, beyond the streets ever so busy, into a secret world. It is a world where one can escape from the drudgeries of daily life into a cool green paradise, where you, too, can become enraptured by the serene beguilement of such sweet tranquillity.

So, let me open the iron gate, my friend. Please step off the street, out of the bustle and the glare of the sun. Walk back into my serene life beyond the walls; into my garden, lush and green; into the cool of the shade. And please, have a seat . . . there, under the sweet olive tree. Relax for a moment, catch your breath. Allow yourself to relinquish the tensions of the day. Put your mind and heart at ease, while I step inside and prepare us a mint julep — I'm told I make a fine mint julep, you know. Be calm . . . and turn, with me, a page of my life.

Arsenal

*P*art of this complex was originally marked off as an area for the French Army Arsenal on a 1722 map of New Orleans. Later it was given by King Louis xv of France to the Ursuline nuns, as their concession when they arrived in the early settlement to begin their work attending to the military hospital and teaching the children of the colonists. The nuns also were the guardians of eligible young ladies, called casket girls after the small carrying box containing a meager trousseau delivered to them by the French crown. These young women were sent from France to Louisiana to become wives to the many young men who had come before them to build the city of New Orleans and the surrounding areas of this French Colony of Louisiana, so named by the early explorer La Salle in honor of King Louis xiv.

The complex is composed of two lots that have been joined to make one of the Vieux Carré's most lovely spots. Hidden behind a high wall, the great magnolia tree overhangs the banquette, or sidewalk, on the street from behind the garden wall.

The small entry door opens to a shaded grass lawn surrounded by a border of ferns and lush, green tropical perennials. The stately building to the left was designated by Frances Xavier Cabrini — representing the Missionary Sisters of the Sacred Heart — as a Catholic school, from 1904 to 1921. Now the school building is residential and is divided into apartments that overlook the lovely gardens.

Between the shady lawn and the old school is a pool made private by boxwood hedges. Along the wall of the building to the right as we enter are a collection of bromeliads; a pink geranium; a Japanese plum tree, or loquat; and a thick pyracantha vine, heavy with flowers. The bed is planted with sword and maidenhair ferns.

A view from the old schoolhouse gives an unobstructed, comprehensive feel of the space and buildings here. Beneath a balcony, a grouping to color a shadowy area includes hanging pots of bromeliads and begonias and red geraniums.

Deeper into the complex is another small court surrounded by brick walls and shaded by a sycamore tree. The central, circular raised bed is planted with delicate, small pink impatiens and monkey grass and is punctuated by an iron planter thick and overflowing with a large bromeliad. This particularly quiet courtyard becomes a sitting area for relaxing and reading. Plantings in this area include a walking iris, or NEOMARICA, and a splendid ASPLENIUM NIDUS, or bird's-nest fern.

A cast-iron and marble side table boasts two
antique leaden urns planted with red impatiens.
The exotic pink flower of a bromeliad leans out of
its pot into the pathway.

Over the wall is an archaic cistern once used to hold rainwater for the neighboring home. The tall redbud tree, CERCIS CANADENSIS, *is just showing spring leaves.*

*Turning out into the open is the area that once
served as the yard for the old school building of the
complex. This building was the school of Saint
Louis Cathedral and the schoolyard is now sup-
planted with a lovely pool.*

From the gallery of the old school, a wide area of
the compound can be seen: pool, gardens, lawn,
patio, old buildings, flowers, trees, rooftops of the
neighboring structures. The walled side of the pool
area has several small displays of interest, each
designed as a singular composition. One display
includes a bacchanalian face peering through the
English ivy covering to a fountain, shrouded by
assorted ferns including staghorn, maidenhair, and
wood.

Beauregard

In 1855, John Slidell, U.S. congressman and diplomat from the South, built this two-story Edwardian frame structure as a wedding gift for his sister-in-law, Marguerite Caroline Deslonde. That year, Caroline, as she was known, married Pierre Gustave Toutant Beauregard, an American army officer who had already distinguished himself in the Mexican War from 1846 to 1848. They made their home together here.

When Louisiana seceded from the Union, in 1861, Beauregard resigned from the American army to fight for the South, eventually becoming a full general in the Confederate army. His involvement and able leadership in every major campaign of the Civil War gave him the reputation of an illustrious combat commander. But P.G.T. Beauregard suffered more from just the battles during those years: his beloved wife, Caroline, died.

The house was sold after the Civil War, with subsequent owners making alterations to the character of the building. The tiny patio that remains is only a part of the original courtyard, yet provides a lovely, small area for cool relaxation and contemplation.

20

Preceding page:

A full view of the left corner of the area, shaded by the shadow of the tall surrounding walls, reveals the spiky, fanlike fronds of several varieties of palms including Chinese fan, windmill, and sago.

Entering the court from an open walkway, down the left side of the building from the street, a cypress driftwood elbow attached to the brick wall cradles two bromeliads. The top is a wispy gray tillandsia, the bottom a rich-green-and-deep-vermilion NEOREGELIA.

The leaves of another windmill palm catch the afternoon light that streams into the far corner of the patio.

A giant elephant ear, ALOCASIA MACRORRHIZA,
*flourishes in the sun of the same corner; its white
spathe glows in the protected shadow below.*

A low showing from a Japanese maple stands before the leaves of a ginger plant.

Another corner view of the patio shows a large bay window of the house that extends into the court.

The wall of the adjoining property appears monastic. The thick metal cross is positioned there for salvation — the salvation of the wall. The cross anchors a metal rod that bolsters and strengthens the once-sagging wall.

It is appropriate that in this same garden a resurrection fern, now a brown dead-looking fur on an oak branch, waits only for the next rain before it comes alive again to resemble a furry green coat. A single camellia blooms its pink flower.

The view from within the house out into the secret garden provides a painting of greens and light, both close and far. The sky holds another reminder of the Creole life here: the steeple of a nearby French Quarter church.

Begue

❦

In 1853, Philip Kettering and his sister Elizabeth arrived in New Orleans from their native
Germany. Philip worked as a butcher in the
French Market and soon met Louis Dutrey, a
butcher from Gascony, France. When Philip brought Louis
home to meet his sister, Louis became entranced: he soon
asked Philip for her hand in marriage. After the marriage,
they opened a small, single-dining-room restaurant on
an upstairs floor near the corner of Madison and Decatur
streets called Dutrey's. The eatery became a favorite
among the butchers of the French Market.

The butchers had long been an influential group in the
market. Years before, a Frenchman named Robin, traveling
through the city between 1803 and 1805, commented in his
papers:

> Many individuals practice themselves (or have practiced
> by their slaves) the trade of butcher. In no other country
> in the world do the inhabitants eat so much meat. The
> Louisianian deserves the title of "carnivore." Everywhere
> on the table one finds small pieces of bread and large
> pieces of meat. The children eat so much of it that a
> European would fear for their health, but they grow tall
> and vigorous and appear perfectly healthy. . . . Vegeta-
> bles are found only on the tables of the rich. Meat is the
> food of everyone.

> Thus, there are many butchers doing a good business.
> Business is so brisk at their stalls in the market that they
> are sold out by eight or nine o'clock in the morning.
> (C. C. Robin, *Voyage to Louisiana, 1803–1805,* trans.
> Stuart O. Landry [New Orleans: Pelican Publishing,
> 1966], 37)

When Louis Dutrey died in 1875, Elizabeth kept the restaurant open with the help of her able friend Hypolite Begue. Elizabeth eventually married Begue and changed the name of their restaurant to Begue's. They prospered and gained international notoriety in 1884, the year of the Cotton Centennial in New Orleans. A little book printed in 1900 describing some of Madame Begue's recipes recounts the experience: "But you mount the stairs, and are thrust, as it were, into an atmosphere of succulent herbs and redolent peppers. You have passed the narrow portals and lo, are ushered into that particular and peculiar domain presided over by that genius of Epicurus — that saint of gourmet and gourmand — Madame Begue."

Elizabeth Kettering Dutrey Begue died in 1906 and Monsieur Begue in 1917, which marked the close of the restaurant. This was their home on Bourbon Street and is the location of this fine secret garden.

This fine building demands attention with an unusually opulent display of greenery on the exterior balcony — just a hint of what lies beyond. The large structure also has a large back house, the slave quarter, that serves as several apartments. The tall magnolia in the center of the courtyard shades the entire garden. The view to the left shows the variety of plantings: azaleas, ferns, gardenias, and impatiens.

Silhouetted is an unusual life-sized deer topiary, standing in the shade. Another unusual topiary, grown into the shape of a monkey, swings in the breeze over a soft bed of white impatiens.

A wide view toward the back house shows the tall potted cherry laurels and the flagstone surface, which has been laid onto the bare earth with space between the stones where tiny ferns and welcomed grasses can thrive.

Through the solarium door of the front house is a view of an assortment of greenery, statuary, and a swimming pool. This L-shaped pool hugs the wall of the right border of the court. The wall itself is latticed and hung with baskets of white impatiens.

The full view of the courtyard from the pool side delineates the areas of plantings and flagstones. Almost every flower in this garden is white, enhancing and lightening the deep greens of the abundant foliage. The small elephant topiary stands atop a rose marble table . . .

35

while mighty stone torsos uphold great boughs of fern and petunias, with azaleas and gardenias at their feet.

A high wall in a shaded corner holds baskets of white petunias and staghorn fern, white and pink impatiens, and other autonomous ferns that have determined their own location.

This small courtyard is a precious jewel, or BIJOU, *as the French would say it. From the unpretentious entryway on the street, the court is entered down a side corridor and through the iron gate. Old bricks have been laid down in half-circle and herringbone patterns to enhance the ground*

Bijou

One of the delights of the gardens in this collection is their variety of size. This little garden, though one of the smallest of the group, is one of the most charming. The little house that claims this jewel is again located on a lot that was originally assigned to the arsenal of the French army in 1722 and was later given to the Ursuline nuns by brevet of King Louis xv of France. The land given to the nuns was substantial within the over-all scheme of the small settlement because their wide range of duties required ample space. Not only did the Ursulines care for the sick in the army hospital and teach the young girls of the colony, but they were extremely involved with medicine, herbal treatment of disease, and botany. A large part of their land was given over to an herbal garden where the nuns grew and experimented with local herbs as well as those brought here for cultivation from Europe and the Caribbean Islands.

When the Ursulines sold their land and moved their convent and school to another part of New Orleans, much of the area was divided into lots and sold to home builders seeking permanent residences. The home here, which dates from 1836, was found in such terrible repair when its renovations began in 1968 that the new owners had a unique opportunity in that even the courtyard required complete renovation, landscaping, and planting.

surface. A stone boy holding a goose is fountain-head for the small semicircular brick pond along the way. The tall leaves of ASPIDISTRA ELATIOR *provide his hiding place; a sprinkling of pink impatiens adds a splash of bright color to this cool spot.*

The walk continues underneath the balcony of the
L-shaped building into the open patio. Handsome
wrought-iron furniture provides a dining area
decorated with a basket of orange-flowered kalanchoe, bromeliad, and English ivy.

The central fountain splashes delicately, drawing attention to a border of variegated LIGUSTRUM; *pink, white, and red geraniums; and pink impatiens behind.*

A white-cluster flower of bridal wreath, SPIRAEA VANHOUTTEI, *sways in the slight breeze.*

A ray of sunlight reaches down into the shade to illuminate a blooming flower of a variegated ginger plant, and two lovely white lilies reach up through the foliage. The statue in the rear of the court lingers quietly as company to garden visitors.

From the rear of the court, the view forward is beautiful. This patio truly captures the essence of a Vieux Carré courtyard.

To the right, the heavy, pale pink blooms of a PRUNUS ACCOLADE *stand tall against the neigh-boring wall. A stone boy standing above the dusty miller and pink begonias guard the serenity of this French Quarter* BIJOU.

Bouligny

*I*n 1769, when New Orleans was transferred from French to Spanish possession, Commandant Don Alessandro O'Reilly arrived with an impressive army of three thousand soldiers. One of these soldiers was Don Francisco Bouligny. O'Reilly was not the first to arrive in the name of Spain, however. He had been recently preceded by Don Antonio de Ulloa, who was unsuccessful in wresting government control from the French colonists. They believed that France would regain dominion over the land.

When O'Reilly arrived at the Belize — the term given the mouth of the Mississippi at the Gulf of Mexico — he sent Bouligny upriver to the city to ascertain the attitude of its citizens. Bouligny found them willing to submit to Spanish rule, having by then finally become convinced that France would not intervene on their behalf.

When O'Reilly was assured of a successful Spanish domination, he left the colony and Bouligny behind. Bouligny had that year married Louise d'Auberville, daughter of the marine commissioner of Louisiana, and he remained in Louisiana. Bouligny was eventually appointed acting governor. His son and grandson became statesmen and left a time-honored Louisiana legacy in the name Bouligny.

In the location of this secret garden, Don Francisco Bouligny and his wife, Louise, once made their home. In 1810, the existing building was erected and remains one of the oldest structures in the Vieux Carré, having two small patios and a rooftop terrace. The property also has the distinction of being owned by an art dealer who appreciates her artistic environment in the gardens as well as in the building itself, where she and her husband live and operate a small, exclusive art gallery.

Preceding page:

Through the iron gates of a side driveway — a luxury in the Vieux Carré —stands the high wall of a neighboring building that holds a collection of staghorn ferns. The brick bed, running the length of the wall to a back court, is planted with Mexican heather, brimming with tiny purple flowers, and ferns. A swell of giant elephant ears fills the corner space, which turns into the first court of the property.

A look into this first court reveals an elaborate cast-iron bench, painted a deep green, which blends with the leaves of the PHILODENDRON SEL-LOUM *standing behind. The arched iron gate to the left opens to a walk that tunnels through a back slave-quarter building to another court. This back court is enclosed by high walls, allowing a thin shaft of light to enter, which moves across the area as the day passes.*

In this back court, which contains a fountain in the arch against the side wall, there is a great deal of humidity, which contributes to the health and growth of the many fern varieties here. A lovely holly fern, rooted directly in the wall, grows near the fountain. Another wall displays a selection of bromeliads above and a FATSIA JAPONICA, or Japanese Aralia, below.

A palette of plastered and exposed brick displays a metal weatherproof artwork, balanced by a variety of ferns in the wall, to the left, with wisteria and pyracantha above.

Above the slave quarters there is a terrace, most often used for entertaining, barbecues, and cocktail parties. A magnolia rises from the court between the front and back buildings.

Through the wall of the terraced area is a small barred arch, only large enough to view rising smoke from oncoming fires, which were calamitous to the city in 1788 and 1794. From the terrace view, a tall banana from a neighboring patio hangs its flower and early fruit into the court below.

Another exterior artwork — an ocher shield face — guards the tranquillity of this secret garden.

Bourbon

The space and size of Vieux Carré lots were determined by the French, as was their practice of building directly on the banquette, or sidewalk, securing privacy in the courts and gardens behind their primary living quarters. The French also possessed the Gallic sentiment of desire for privacy in the home. The original front houses were smaller than today's Spanish-influenced homes, with larger garden areas for growing vegetables and raising poultry and farm animals to feed the family; but as the buildings were replaced either because of the great fires, or the fashion, or the fortunes of the property owner, interior space increased and exterior space decreased. Land use changed. Due to the success of New Orleans as a port, no longer did the growing number of wealthy merchants occupying the inner city have to rely upon their gardens for provisions. The French Market, only blocks away from any residence, was flourishing with the growth of the city. As the market provided the French and Spanish cooks in the city the foodstuffs to develop a cuisine native to the area, the wealth and imagination of landowners allowed a new, indigenous architecture to develop: French in concept, Spanish in design.

The court of this property is behind a magnificent residence located on famed Bourbon Street. Bourbon Street was not named for the whiskey of that appellation but for the Bourbon-Orleans family, rulers of France, of which Louis XIV and the Duc d'Orleans were members.

The stately courtyard of this 1795 building is entered by a porte cochere from the street. The porte cochere is a carriageway that was built through the building, wide and high enough for the family carriage to enter — tall-hatted driver and all. At the end of the carriageway is an altar with a Spanish Virgin, Madonna of the Roses. This was a once-common sight in old New Orleans courtyards. The high arched entrance provides a view of the entire court.

Through the garden to the rear slave quarter, the jungle of trees and plants is designed to be appreciated as a whole, rather than to be viewed as individual plantings. A view from the slave-quarter balcony through the trees, which include a magnolia to the right, reveals the fountain and glassed high archways on two floors of the main building. These archways were originally open to the grand interior stair and landings, which now serve as interior space.

A closer view of one arch beneath a datura branch and past the fountain reflects the balcony of the rear building.

A crowded corner contains a palmetto, an important indigenous Louisiana species.

The cast-iron fountain drips water tranquilly into beds of water hyacinths. The water hyacinth, or Richardson lily — EICHHORNIA CRASSIPES — is a water plant found in many Vieux Carré fountains and ponds. Its delicate purple flowers and fleshy reptilian leaves add to the exotic collection of Louisiana plantings.

Of specific note are the white-painted cast-iron chairs and benches found in this garden. They were popular designs made in Paris in the 1840s, few of which made it as far as New Orleans. Because of their unusual and elaborate designs, these pieces have been copied by a local ironworks as patterns for manufacture.

At the exit door on the street, a cast-iron grille serves as a look-through to Bourbon Street outside and the bright sun of midday.

Briquette

The first buildings constructed in New Orleans were wood frame with cypress shingles —barely more than protective huts. Historically, the next group of buildings were of *bousillage,* a mixture of mud and moss that was formed into walls and allowed to dry and harden. This indigenous Louisiana moss was called Spanish beard by the French, and French wig by the Spanish. It was the moss we now call Spanish moss, *Tillandsia usneoides.* It is not a parasite but attaches itself to other plants. This plant draws water and dust from the air; that is all it needs to survive. It is found here mostly in oak and cypress trees.

Later in the development of the city, when things were becoming more economically stable and buildings needed to be more durable, the most common building method became *briquette-entre-poteaux,* or bricked-between-posts, construction. In this method, wood posts, cut from cypress, would be set crisscross standing up from the ground to form the frame of the walls. The bricks were then fitted into the spaces and cemented with mortar.

The first bricks to be used here were made from a red sand found at the crescent of the river. The hardened bricks were not as hard as the bricks in use today, but they served their purpose. The mortar was the key to the success of this construction method. It was made from a mixture that included the dust of burned clam shells, which formed a firmer bond than many newer products. The recipe for the mixture is lost, but many of the walls made this way are standing today in the Vieux Carré. Because of the softness of the red bricks, it was necessary for the walls to be plastered. This is why the bricked-between-posts construction is not visible to the eye in our structures.

The patio is entered through an elaborate iron gate past beds of red geraniums.

After the great fires in 1788 and 1794 destroyed almost all of the city, bricks were sold at a premium. The government, as well as the people, desired more substantial buildings, and brick was the preferred material. As time passed, harder bricks began to be imported into the city. These harder bricks allowed the construction of larger buildings, many of which dominate the French Quarter today.

The location of this secret garden was the main brickyard in the city. It was centrally located but never had any substantial or architecturally significant structures built on it. In the twentieth century, as construction supply stores were moved to locations with larger storage areas, the brickyard moved and a home was built here — a brick home, of course.

There is a large open patio, also bricked, and walls of brick that surround the area.

A wide view of the patio shows the house to the left, built at the rear of the property rather than directly on the street, as are most Vieux Carré properties. A table near the fountain against the wall is used for alfresco dining.

Around the fountain area are thick plantings of bananas. A single early flower shoots up through the mass of fleshy green leaves. Several varieties of canna share one bed: a large double orange canna flower stands aside a red CANNA IRIDIFLORA.

In the center of the patio stands one of the largest magnolia trees in the French Quarter. A ground area beneath it has been left for its roots to breathe, where a grouping of bromeliads, dracaena, spider plant, and garden elves shares the space. Leaves of a variegated ginger extend into the path.

One wall is covered with a giant pathos vine,
while another is home to a hanging basket of
bird's-nest fern — ASPLENIUM NIDUS.

In a corner of the patio grows a fig tree. The pelican, Louisiana's state bird, stands quiet . . .

74

close to a sago palm. A vigilant kitten watches
over the patio from a soft bed of pink ageratum.

Conflagration

The Vieux Carré suffered two disastrous fires during the Spanish domination, which virtually destroyed all the original buildings. Governor Don Estevan Miro described the first fire in his dispatch to the Spanish Court:

> On the 21st of March, 1788, being Good Friday, at half past one in the afternoon, a fire broke out in New Orleans, in the house of the Military Treasurer . . . and reduced to ashes eight hundred and fifty-six edifices, among which were the stores of all the merchants, and the dwellings of the principal inhabitants, the Cathedral, the Convent of the Capuchins, with the greater portion of their books, the Townhall, the watch-house, and the arsenal with all its contents. . . . Almost the whole of the population of the smouldering town was ruined and deprived even of shelter during the whole of the following night. (Charles Gayarre, *History of Louisiana.* Volume 3, 3d Ed. [New Orleans: Armand Hawkins, 1885], 203, 204)

It had happened that the bells of the Catholic Church of the Capuchins, which also served as alarm bells, were not sounded due to the regulations of the good fathers that the bells remain silent on Good Friday, the day observed as the anniversary of Jesus Christ's death. One spectator who had experienced the tragedy firsthand commented, "A civilized nation is not made to adopt maxims so culpable towards humanity, and this trait of fanatical insanity will surely not be approved by sensible people" (Grace King, *New Orleans, the Place and the People* [New York: Macmillan, 1895], 131).

Six years and eight and a half months later, another fire occurred. Governor Baron Francois Louis Hector de Carondelet notified the court of Madrid of the fire of December 8, 1794, that

This property, having a deep "key" lot, has a flagged side court, as well as an enclosed "piscine," or pool area, in the rear. Along the wall are several small areas of plantings; an orange-pink hibiscus begins the potted flowers.

a conflagration, but too well favored by a strong north wind, and originating in Royal Street, through the imprudence of some children playing on the court-yard . . . which was adjacent to a hay store, had consumed in three hours two hundred and twelve of the most valuable dwellings and magazines, the property of private individuals, as well as edifices of the greatest value belonging to the government. (Charles Gayarre, *History of Louisiana,* vol. 3, 3d ed. [New Orleans: Armand Hawkins, 1885], 335)

In his dispatch, the governor recommended that the Crown give "premiums" to those rebuilding the destroyed properties "with terraced roofs, or with roofs made of tile instead of [cypress wood] shingles as formerly" (ibid., 336). These premiums were probably in the form of a relaxation of taxes levied on imported Spanish roofing tiles and perhaps even further reduction of taxes on the structure and lot.

Devastating as these fires were to the burgeoning — then Spanish — town of New Orleans, they consecutively cleared away many inferior, ill-constructed buildings and impressed the residents that it was essential to erect more substantial, fire-resistant structures.

The buildings standing today are the result. They are far more grand than their predecessors. There is an undeniable elegance in them, resulting from their Spanish, not French, architecture.

Farther along is a grouping that includes orange and yellow hardy amaryllis in the bed, a morning glory vine to the left, a small bromeliad and asparagus fern to the right.

A bricked rectangular fountain boasts a statue overseeing iris, elephant ear, and potted coleus.

Nearby, against the brick wall, is a collection of potted pink, magenta, and red impatiens and a variegated privet. A red kalanchoe flower glows from under the shadows.

The pool area is separated by an antique cast-iron fence, painted rusty pink.

A MAHONIA BEALEI *grows to one side, its prickly leaves best not touched, while a bright yellow iris bloom contrasts with its own dark green leaves. A small cast-iron fountain hangs on the wall, probably brought here by an early group of Germans, who came to farm some of the nearby plantations.*

In the rear there is a latticed sitting area and a statue of a maiden watching the fountain. Hibiscus, dusty miller, and croton border the pool.

A view back toward the house shows the shuttered windows and doors, balconied second story, and dormer window in the attic area, as well as the corridor exit to the street. All are signatures of French Quarter architecture.

Heguy

The Vieux Carré survives today as one of America's most well preserved architectural places. The history of the city is spoken in every facade of every building that hugs the banquette, or sidewalk, or relies on the common wall of the next structure for mutual succor and support. The Vieux Carré is a living and thriving city within a city. The charm and quaint attitude of the eighteenth- and nineteenth-century buildings is preserved alongside other buildings of equal enchantment that were built in the twentieth century, in accord with the design and *tout ensemble* of this vicinity.

However, the French Quarter was not always as healthy as it is today. In the 1920s and into the early 1930s, the Vieux Carré was suffering a decay that almost destroyed it. Other than for the few proud old Creole families — the direct descendants of the French and Spanish who built New Orleans — who lived in and maintained their ancestral homes and businesses, the architecture of the locale was fast deteriorating due to the poverty of the owners or disinterest in the area at a time when it was no longer fashionable. The city had grown rapidly since the 1870s, and newer areas had become the seat of commerce. Many choice residences were being built in the emerging vogue neighborhoods.

It was during the 1930s that a group of concerned citizens, residents of the Vieux Carré, banded together and formed what is today called the Vieux Carré Commission. The purpose of the commission was to spearhead a drive to turn back the deterioration and advancing destruction of the French Quarter and to preserve the *tout ensemble* of the rare architectural treasures of the area. Today the French Quarter —.through the work of the Vieux Carré Commission and the many property owners who have spent a great deal of time, money, and effort through the years in piecing

Today, the walk through the house brings us to the entrance of the garden, which is unique in several ways. Its extended depth has allowed the owners to develop several separate areas or environments, offering multiple attitudes. The seasoned brick surfacing and high bordering walls render an ambience of antiquity, while the pool defers to our contemporary culture. The pool, designed as a lap pool for exercise as well as a decorative oasis, was built to fit inside the diminutive width of the area while still allowing space for a small contemporary pool cottage.

The wall along the right of the court is planted with several trees and shrubs. A flower of the FEIJOA SELLOWIANA, a pineapple guava, is already blooming its smooth white petals with purple stamens touched in yellow.

the French Quarter back together — is a beautiful and unusual place.

The neighborhood of this residence was one that included small, unpretentious homes that were generally occupied by laborers of the early city. The record books show that in 1811, this building was passed in ownership by a gentleman of the city to one Alexandrine Heguy, "f.w.c.," or free woman of color.

The building is fabricated of the antiquated *briquette-entre-poteaux* construction and is now enrobed in a lively chemise of yellow plaster. The home is not a large one, measuring only 32 feet in width, but it is located on a lot in its city block that was once designated a "key" lot. The key lots of each block, of which there were two, were situated in the center of each square and spanned equally into the full depth of the block's center, backing up to one another. This lot of approximately 160 feet in depth is as long as any in the French Quarter. Another two-story back building, a fatality of time, once housed a kitchen and quarters for the servants.

Against the wall at the end of the pool grows a Cape Honeysuckle, TECOMARIA CAPENSIS, *its orange blossoms just beginning to share the summer light.*

The view back through the garden, framed by the branches of a redbud tree, looks across the pool, where lush foliage overhangs the water. An arrangement of potted white, pink, and red geraniums brightens a corner of the brick path.

To the right, a small domain has been designated as a sitting area with an interesting variety of greenery. The farthest corner boasts PILEA, *Mexican heather, in the low beds; a young althaea, or rose of Sharon; and a honeysuckle vine climbing the wall to the right.*

The plump green pods of a datura will open to become beautiful white angel trumpets. A low table is set with purple and white petunias and a small copper watering can.

A single magnificent red rose hangs heavy from its stem.

Immigrant

During periods in which the French Quarter was shunned by New Orleanians as the unfashionable place to live, its structures were left to fall into decay and, sometimes, destruction. During these times the poorest of the populace — the newest arrivals from foreign shores — would inhabit these buildings.

Ironically, it was because of the destitution of these people that the buildings, in many cases, remain today. Rather than having the wherewithal to raze a building, or even to alter it architecturally in major ways, these people were forced to make do with what existed and to accept the conditions of their homes as adequate. Improvements consisted principally of fixing the roof of leaks and maintaining the shell of the building sufficiently enough to provide the family with protection from the elements. In effect, the integrity of the engineering and design of the structure were preserved.

In the early 1900s, many Italians, coming from Sicily and other areas, made up the greatest number of that period's infusion of immigrants. Arriving in the Creole City, they relied on trades familiar to them, such as fishing, farming, and the purveyance of vegetables. They virtually overtook the French Market and became the principal vegetable and produce vendors of New Orleans. Soon, they became able to purchase many of the properties in the Vieux Carré that had been originally built by the French and the Spanish. The area of the French Quarter bordering the French Market became almost entirely populated by these resourceful, hardworking Italian families.

Because of this cultural phenomenon, this home remains architecturally intact today; its small, interesting courtyard reflects in its plantings the feeling of the original design.

A view through the courtyard from the entryway of the house shows an impressive grouping of tropical, leafy green flora from lady palms, or RHAPIS, *and yucca on the left, to giant elephant ear and banana on the right. Hanging from the balcony are baskets of spider plant, fern, and bromeliads.*

A closer look at the collection to the left identifies a sago palm; a tall yucca; an asparagus fern in the planter on top of the white column; and a NEANTHE BELLA *palm,* CHAMAEDOREA ELEGANS, in the white cast-iron urn on the flagstone surface. This tall variety of yucca is called a Spanish dagger. It is often used, as in the past, as a discouragement to intruders who might venture climbing over the wall into the privacy of a patio.

An aloe vera is located where it can catch a slim ray of garden sunlight. The nineteenth-century wire chair, a souvenir of a previous age, is a prize found by the owner of this property along the riverfront wharves.

A cast-iron love seat is hidden
among the palms.

A collection of wall plants includes spider plant, bromeliads, and pothos surrounding a small cast-iron fountain. The familiar olla, the huge Spanish olive oil jar, serves as a decorative planter and reminder of the Spanish domination of the city.

The arched door that enters the patio is also Spanish in design. Light filters into the court and the upper-floor balcony on which stand several yucca.

At the wall of an old chimney stands a rusted iron cemetery gate, surrounded by Swedish ivy, ginger, and a small potted spider plant.

Giant elephant ear and bananas fill the planter bed along the wall that leads back to the door from which the patio is entered, and an exit is now taken.

Jalousie

This late-eighteenth-century Spanish colonial cottage was built only a few years before the United States took possession of New Orleans as a territory. This little house of *briquette-entre-poteaux* was first erected with a one-story front house and a two-story rear kitchen, a separate structure. The small area between the two is the patio, which now serves as the interior/exterior living room of the complex. The two buildings were joined by a third, narrow two-story structure that runs along one side of the court from the front to the back buildings. Erected in the mid-twentieth century, this middle building expanded the indoor interiors of the property advantageously.

During the Spanish colonial period of New Orleans, government officials were forced by necessity to find new ways to tax people and, at one time, levied a tax on every interior closet and staircase in residential structures. For this reason, there are no interior closets authentic to the original design of this building complex. It was because of this closet tax that the armoire, a large wooden cabinet holding one's entire wardrobe, became popular. Since interior stairs were also taxed, many stairs, as are these, were built on the exterior of the edifice. This house was built by a white Creole gentleman for his illegitimate quadroon daughter, whose mother was an enchanting and exquisite mulattress and mistress to the father.

The building is of Haitian design, built by a free Haitian of color who had come to New Orleans as a refugee from slave uprisings in his own country. The buildings originally housed a *boulangerie* (bread baker's shop) and residence in the front and an unconnected *garçonnière* in the rear. The *garçonnière* served as living area for the male progeny of the family so that they would have their privacy from the females. In these times, the sons of a family were allowed an indulgence of freedom while the daughters were over-protected and chaperoned every moment, until they were given away into a marriage or fixed in some other acceptable arrangement.

The entryway to today's cottage is at the right of the property. The sea-foam green shutters help maintain the Haitian look of the exterior design, while the dark green door insinuates luxuriant herbage. As you enter the outside door, a fleshy elephant ear crouches happily in the corner of the doorway leading into the house. On entering the house, the focus of one's attention is dominated by the view through the doors opening onto the courtyard.

The small courtyard is treated as an interior living room as much as an exterior one. The surrounding buildings and walls keep it cool in the hottest of summer days, while the warmth of those same buildings repels the chill of winter's low temperatures. The banana trees and the fish-tail palm line the walls to the left. A view across the patio to the rear building exposes philodendron, yucca, and bromeliads. To the other side is a Chinese fan palm, LIVISTONA CHINENSIS. There is an openness to this small enclosure.

The back rose-colored wall holds a small collection
of bromeliads, while an exterior jalousied stair and
balcony hide the spaces behind. The jalousie looks
like wide shutters. They were designed to secure
privacy while admitting the breeze to pass
through. Other potted tropicals include tall skele-
tal bamboo, sago palm, and SCHEFFLERA. The
amber cast of a verdigris wall sconce illuminates
the tinkling waters of the tiny fountain and the
plants below.

Seen through a window of the upper-floor bed-
room, as well as a louvered shutter, the tops of the
bananas stand tall, tattered by the breeze. Another
door lends a peek at the entrance to a neighboring
house, colors, stairs, and shutters: shades of
another time.

Mercantile

There is a variety in both use and design in all of the French Quarter buildings. This grand building with its comparatively large courtyard once housed a stable with room enough in the rear for dray carts, as well as a wide carriageway where elegant carriages could be parked. During the Spanish colonial period of New Orleans, from 1769 to 1803, only a single Spanish design cart was allowed to be used for drayage in the city. It was chosen by the officials because it made a great deal of noise, which made it difficult to cart untaxed goods without detection through the streets to and from the ships waiting at the quay for import or export.

This substantial edifice was built to house a large commercial enterprise on the ground floor; there were also balconied upper-floor residences and back buildings in the rear housing stables, additional second-floor residences, and storage. The building has, in the past, served as a location for a grocery and a winery depot. Today, the entire complex has been transformed into residential areas with apartments of various layouts and sizes. The front apartments offer a view of the street below, as well as an overview of the court behind. This wide court has been surfaced with cement, with brick beds along the outer wall.

From the street, one passes through two sets of massive gates to the interior courtyard. The tall banana trees, their leaves swaying in the breeze, create a tropical feeling.

The young althaea, or rose of Sharon, partially shaded by the overhang of the balcony, yields two lavender blooms.

The view into the court from the slave-quarter balcony allows an overview of the entire court.

The wide-spreading FICUS CARICA, or fig tree, is heavy with early green fruit. The fig is one of the trees that came to the colony from the Mediterranean with the Ursulines and the Jesuits.

The fig fruits profusely in New Orleans. When ripe, the fruit is harvested and made into delicious jams, preserves, and wine, as well as pies and ice cream.

At the far rear of the garden is a stairway leading to the upper floor of the slave quarters of the back building. In years past, many homes had quarters attached for the household servants and their families. Throughout the Vieux Carré, these buildings have now been elegantly renovated into some of the most posh residences of the district.

On the wall by the stair is a charmingly grouped arrangement of impatiens in whites and varying shades of pink, with rose and green caladiums that brighten the somber gray patina of the cement covering on the wall.

Moving back into the court, a grouping of plantings consists of orange and white impatiens, bananas, yucca, Japanese yew, and bird of paradise. Through the courtyard, toward the street, the Spanish arches of the fan window on the second floor and of the portico are visible.

Bananas, white impatiens, and small elephant ears surround a large and rare sugar caldron, once used to boil sweet thick juice crushed out of the all-important sugarcane into a syrup. This remaining vessel stands as evidence of an industry that saved the early settlement from bankruptcy and turned a troubled and dying colony into a thriving economic phenomenon, leading the world in production of sugar for many years to come. The caldron now exists as a fountain with a single fount that gently adds a note of calm to the sounds of the court. It is a place for goldfish to live, for visiting birds to bathe and refresh themselves before moving on in their busy, frantic lives.

A healthy sword fern holds tight against the wall from which it grows.

The yellows and oranges of a lantana peek out
from under the shade. A painted tile plaque on the
wall, a souvenir from the Spanish era, remains as
tribute to the Catholic influence of past cultures.

Orleans

This secret garden on the Rue d'Orleans, or Orleans Street, is entered by a side corridor and a lacy wrought-iron gate. The unusual lavender color of the building gives a relaxed feel to the bricked courtyard. A first splash of floral color comes from this orange-yellow snapdragon.

nusual in color and marvelous in design is this secret garden located on Orleans Street. When the plan for the city of New Orleans was drawn up by Le Blond de la Tour, he was instructed to name important streets after the French royalty and their patron saints. The Rue d'Orleans was named after the Orleans faction of the Bourbon royal family, and the city was named after Philip II, Duc d'Orleans, regent of France, and brother of the recently deceased Louis XIV. In 1715, Louis XV was not quite ready to take the throne at his great-grandfather's death: he was only five years old. Until he reached the age of thirteen — his legal majority — his uncle Philip, Duc d'Orleans, acted as regent.

In a letter dated April 14, 1721, sent by Adrien de Pauger, assistant to de la Tour and the engineer actually on location laying out the city, de Pauger wrote for approval of some changes:

> [The land] being higher on the river bank, I have brought the town site and the locations marked for the houses of the principle inhabitants closer to it, so as to profit from the proximity of the landing place as well as to have more air from the breezes that come from it. I have likewise indicated the distribution of some of the lots of the plan . . . in order to proportion them to the faculties of the inhabitants and of such size that each and every one may have the houses on the street front and may still have some land in the rear to have a garden, which here is half of life. (Samuel Wilson, Jr., *The Vieux Carré New Orleans: Its Plan, Its Growth, Its Architecture* [New Orleans: Historic District Demonstration Study Report, Bureau of Governmental Research, 1968], 12)

The streets in New Orleans were laid out to best answer the climatic realities of this southern location. So that the heat would not become too severe in the summer, the streets were measured at a width of only thirty-eight feet, in order that the buildings themselves would be shaded by one another. Orleans Street, however, was laid out at a width of forty-five feet as the central grand rue of the city.

Nearby, a red impatiens shares a spot with a wandering Jew. Farther into the court, a comfortable corner serves as a dining and lounging area aside a trickling fountain. Variegated ginger, elephant ear, and crepe myrtle fill out the corner.

Lower, in the same corner, is a mixture of more variegated ginger, a rhoeo vine with pink flowers, Mexican heather with tiny purple flowers, white pansies, yellow marigolds, and purple violas.

To the side of the entrance to the patio is a grouping containing THUNBERGIA vine, impatiens, geraniums, begonias, dusty miller, and Johnny-jump-ups. A beautiful walking iris — NEOMARICA NORTHIANA — reaches its beautiful white-and-purple flower out into the court.

A small pink begonia sits aside a large strawberry
pot with side planters, now home to sweet alyssum and English ivy. A nephthytis vine climbs
the wall of the impressive exterior stair to the
upper floor of the home and slave quarters. From
the balcony of the slave quarters the taller trees are
more visible. There is althaea to the left and a
crepe myrtle to the right.

A freestanding iron gate partitions the court into two defined areas, while in the shadows a kalanchoe flower's fiery red color burns upward from the variety of green leaves below. Next to the red kalanchoe is a yellow snapdragon.

At the rear of the front house is a bay of windows that allows a full view of the court from the interior of the building. In this small room, it is possible to enjoy the courtyard at all times, no matter what the weather or temperature may be.

This court is unusually spacious, and the simplicity of its plantings maintains that openness.

The balcony provides a full view of the court. It is easy to imagine La Petite Patti coming out from her rooms, through the magnificent Spanish door on the second story of the house, to the landing where her guests, gathered in the court below, would raise their glasses in a toast to her latest performance. She would greet them all from her perch, then descend into the court to greet guests individually.

Patti

This court, more open than most in the Vieux Carré, has a dramatic history. In 1777, it was acquired in a partnership by Antoine Cavelier, a descendant of Robert Cavelier, Sieur de la Salle, the man who claimed the lands of the Mississippi Valley, including Louisiana, for King Louis XIV of France. The current structure was built by Antoine around 1789. Buildings on the property before that time were destroyed by the first great fire in New Orleans, in 1788, one that nearly leveled the entire city. Miraculously, this edifice survived the second great fire, in 1794, and is one of the oldest buildings in the Vieux Carré.

A more romantic aspect of the courtyard's history is that the building was once occupied by the young coloratura soprano Adelina Patti, who was born in Madrid in 1843 as Adela Juana Maria Patti. La Petite Patti, as she was known in New Orleans, had sung concerts in New York from the age of seven, making her opera debut there in 1859 as Lucia in Gaetano Donizetti's *Lucia di Lammermoor.* She and her sister Amalia; Amalia's husband; and Adelina's director, Maurice Strakosch, arrived in New Orleans soon after to sing in the French Opera House here. Tradition has it that the opening performance of the theater had disappointed patrons of the opera thoroughly, and financial ruin seemed in sight for the opera house. However, La Petite Patti sang in *Lucia di Lammermoor* and thrilled the music lovers of New Orleans. Her continued successes in a repertoire of seven favored operas made her the toast of the town. Her rooms and court became one of the great social rendezvous of the time. Many gatherings were held in the court to honor her. Upon leaving New Orleans, Adelina Patti performed at Covent Garden in London, where she won the hearts of opera lovers, as she had in New Orleans.

The entrance to the court from the street is through a portico of Spanish design. Its rounded arch and exterior stair to the upper floor, or ÉTAGE — as the New Orleans French called the second floor — are typical of buildings constructed during the Spanish domination of the city.

The herringbone-bricked court is enhanced by a welcoming show of yellow daylilies, above which stands a terra-cotta urn displaying a feathery green asparagus fern. To the right corner of the patio, behind the fern and lilies, stands a large ERY-THRINA, also called a coral, or lobster claw, tree.

Its pink, waxy, birdlike buds hang like a display of tiny Chinese lanterns.

The center of the rear of the court is neatly punctuated with a white wood and wrought-iron bench, behind which rises a magnificent ALPINIA SPECIOSA, *or shell ginger shrub, in full bloom.*

The unusual flowers dangle like necklaces of
seashells or clusters of pale grapes, with the larger
buds of each cluster unfolding to reveal the canary
and scarlet inner blossoms.

A requisite patch of giant bananas, leaves tattered
from the river's breezes, stands to shade the court.

In another corner a huge-leafed ALOCASIA, or giant elephant ear, enjoys the subtropical clime. A very tall loquat tree rises high above the second-floor building, reaching almost to the top of the three-story structure behind. A patinated wall, rich in mauve and pink, supports an English ivy and the smaller-leafed claw vine.

The plantings remain simple, leaving the space refreshingly open for the French Quarter. Adelina Patti's fame will live on in this Royal Street court.

144

Reconstruction

The minor buildings existing on this property were razed in 1865 to accommodate the construction of this home. The plans were laid out clearly in a contract written between the owner of the lot and a contractor named Frank Guitare, who accepted the job for $4,500.00 and signed the contract with his *x* mark. The adjoining homes were occupied on one side by a free Negress, and on the other by a free woman of color. This historical record is a reminder of the quadroon and octoroon society that once enjoyed a mysterious and elegant existence in New Orleans. However, the struggle to reach this position was an arduous one.

In 1724, the *Code Noir,* or black code, was promulgated in New Orleans and the rest of Louisiana. In this civil code, designed to regulate the slaves and their masters' treatment of them, it was stipulated that marriage between whites and blacks was strictly prohibited. The obvious evidence of miscegenation — mulatto children — was appearing in New Orleans as well as on the plantations. However, children resulting from the marriage of blacks, or *gens de couleur* — people of color — inherited the status of the mother.

The master of a slave had the right to give that slave his or her freedom. If the mother was a slave, the children were also slaves, yet if the mother was a free Negress or a free woman of color, the children would also be free. These children became the first free society of color in New Orleans.

They grew up not only excluded from the rights of the whites but also removed from the society of the black slaves. As these children became adults and had their own children, grandchildren, and great-grandchildren, the progeny became more and more fair in complexion, until they were often indistinguishable from whites, other than in their reputed possession of exotic beauty. These were the quadroons (one-fourth black) and octoroons (one-eighth black) who became so famous in New Orleans demimonde society.

This garden is located in an area of New Orleans that at one time was primarily inhabited by free women of color, who were often the mistresses of Creole gentlemen who supported them and were forbidden by law to marry them.

The contract that Mr. Frank Guitare, the contractor, signed with his *x* on July 12, 1865, describes the proposed building as follows:

> To be finished in a No. 1 style, it being distinctly understood that the lower portion shall be finished complete, the ceiling to be corniced and a large decorative plaster as centerpiece in the ceiling. A large hall on one side with granite steps, box style for entrance, two windows below, three openings above on the front, four openings on the side and four openings in the rear of the house with iron balcony and top verandah, in addition to this the party of the second part will place the yard, kitchen and outhouses in complete order, shall make a large gateway and gate on one side of dwelling, and fence of separation between the adjoining lot of that side. And the said party of the first part covenant and agrees to pay unto the said party of the second part for the sum of Four Thousand Five Hundred Dollars, lawful money of the United States.

The value of this property today approaches several hundred thousand dollars.

The Civil War had ended on April 9 of the same year, with General Lee of the Confederacy surrendering to General Grant of the Union army at Appomattox. The construction of this building was undoubtedly precipitated by that event and could be considered part of what good may have come from the dismal period of Reconstruction.

A front view of the property shows that it is still maintained as described in the building contract, now shaded by an elm tree. At the rear of the house, plantings in this small courtyard begin with potted pink impatiens and birds of paradise. The planter bed along the back wall of the front building contains white and pink impatiens, azaleas, Japanese yew, caladiums, and a CAMELLIA JAPONICA.

A grouping arranged against the muted pink and blue of the back slave quarter includes pink and white impatiens, geraniums, and an olla of ARDI-SIA JAPONICA, or honeysuckle.

Across the courtyard, the sun shines on a MAGNO-LIA GRANDIFLORA, or Southern magnolia, against a high brick wall of the bordering home.

A handsome pair of black cast-iron chairs and a side table, holding a variegated English ivy, provide a shaded place to sit. The half-moon fountain at the side wall is shaded by wall baskets of pink and white impatiens, ferns, and caladiums. A brace of bronze pigeons tarry in the cool timelessness of this place. A stone child playfully pours water from a jar to fill an eternal well, while the dulcet sound of the tinkling water laughs gently in approval.

Beneath the magnolia is an arrangement of red geraniums, rosemary, and parsley. The upper balcony railing of the slave quarter provides support for a creeping wisteria vine.

An unusually small door, no more than eight inches square, provides a convenient look-through where two neighbors can gossip about the day's happenings.

Sauvient

The complex was originally three lots that were brought together to create the size of this area. This lot was one of the last in the Vieux Carré to be used as an orchard. The garden is in front of the house and walled in from the street side. From the street the privacy of the garden is amplified by the thick pyracantha and wisteria climbing along its crest. The pink flowers of a MANDEVILLA *vine peek out over the gate, flanked by a brace of flowering Bradford pear trees. Once inside the gate, the deep attitude of the garden offers a glamorous and dramatic entrance to the estate.*

Towering oak trees provide shade to the garden generally, yet allow enough sunlight for the growing of many colorful flowers.

This romantic secret garden illustrates much about New Orleans history, and the buildings that surround it are a stunning example of the West Indies influence on the city's architecture.

Located on the original map of New Orleans of 1722 drawn by the engineer de la Tour, ownership of the property changed several times before it was held by Joseph Sauvient, who built the major buildings circa 1804. Sauvient had come from Santo Domingo as a refugee from the riots there in 1791. The slave revolt drove thousands of whites and free persons of color from their home island to Louisiana.

The original Sauvient buildings consisted of an elegant stone and brick house on the banquette, with stables and a two-story West Indian–style slave quarter in the rear. The property was inherited by Madame Sauvient's daughter Camille, who married Major Theodore Lewis. Major Lewis and Camille had two sons, John B. Lewis and Dr. George W. Lewis. When George was about to wed, his fiancée's parents sent her to Paris, separating the two lovers. They had come upon information leading them to believe that George's grandmother had been a free woman of color. It was felt that this was a socially unacceptable situation for their daughter. Heartbroken, George retreated into his medical practice, never to marry or have children. His death in 1919 followed an unhappy life that was later ruled by despondency, depression, and eventually addiction.

Having no children, he left his property solely to his niece Louise, a daughter of his brother, John. Family members contested Louise's right to inherit the property singularly. All became embroiled in bitter legal disputes for the remainder of their lives.

The elegant front house of the property burned in 1816, leaving the stables, slave quarters, and the unusual large front garden area, which was never rebuilt upon.

A significant legend is connected with the existing slave quarter. Joseph Sauvient was Jean Laffite's lawyer. Jean Laffite was the famous pirate who assisted Andrew Jackson in the defense of New Orleans and contributed heroically to his victory at the Battle of New Orleans in 1814. It is said that Sauvient secreted a portion of Laffite's pirate treasure away within the construction of the building, and it is yet undiscovered. At present, however, the owners are content with creating their own treasure in the beauty of this secret garden.

This is surely one of the most lovely gardens in the Vieux Carré, with its myriad of flowering plantings. There are undoubtedly more flowers in this garden than any other in the French Quarter. The owners take great pride and spend several hours each day caring for this green space.

Entering the garden through the brick wall on the street affords a magnificent view of its splendor. From the street wall to the house, the yard is divided into quadrants, partitioned by a cross of walks and a central fountain. The two forward sections are long and bordered with monkey grass. The center of the garden is designated by a quiet fountain, home to goldfish and water plants including a dwarf CYPERUS, or umbrella plant, on the left.

The most magnificent square of the garden provides a bed for roses exclusively, and a plentiful variety. They are carefully tended and produce unusual bursts of color. A hungry black caterpillar enjoys a lunch of orange rose petals.

The back walk passes through a brick entryway draped in English ivy. The walk leads to other areas of the complex where a guest cottage, flanked by towering palms, stands in its own private court.

A show of phlox — red, white, and purple —
brightens a shaded corner. The butterfly wings of
a pink cyclamen appear to flutter up through the
phlox. Batten shutters frame the espaliered Japanese yew, which climbs the wall from a neat
growth of rounded boxwood and white and purple
petunias.

Through a wide arch, an open stair inside the building leads up to the second-floor balcony of the main house. The balcony view of the garden is lovely. Looking over the pale green of a wisteria vine into this garden, shaded by the long branches of a great oak, this is easily a place to sit in a rocking chair and pass many an hour in quiet grace.

Soniat

The Soniat House is now a singularly marvelous small hotel. The walkway through the carriage entrance comes to the high arched openings of the courtyard and to a massive exterior stair that leads up to second-floor guest rooms. A giant anthurium adds a patch of green to the interior of the hallway.

Passersby may admire this handsome building on Rue Chartres. They may remark on its brass and iron trims or the lace curtains at its windows. Yet until the doorbell is sounded and the door is opened by a gentleman wearing a crisp white jacket and small black bow tie, they will not glimpse the lovely courtyard garden that lies beyond the solid carriageway door.

This once-private house and secret garden were built by Joseph Soniat. His father, Guy Soniat du Fossat, was a Frenchman of some means who came to New Orleans in the late 1700s and developed Tchoupitoulas Plantation, thirteen miles upriver from the city. Son Joseph inherited Tchoupitoulas and lived there with his wife and thirteen children.

The journey from country to city was a tiresome one and kept the Soniats on the muddy river road for the better part of an entire day. After arriving in town and attending the theater, the opera, or a soiree given by a friend or relative, the family preferred to remain overnight in the city. They required accommodations of considerable size, and even relatives were hesitant to offer hospitality to such a brood. So Joseph followed the custom of many wealthy planters in the first half of the nineteenth century by providing a city residence, or town house, for his family and himself. It was completed in 1830.

After Joseph's death during the Civil War, the property passed through many hands, suffering degrees of deterioration. In the twentieth century, Madame Louis Felton came into possession of the Soniat residence and converted it into a guesthouse. Her rooms were simple and honest, and when she sold the property, the old house was fortunate to have been discovered by its present owners.

The courtyard's function changed over the years. In earlier times, the Soniats' horses were harnessed here, then led down the street for stabling while the family was in town. A small carriage remained with a brace of horses at the ready for evening engagements. Parts of the inner courtyard were partitioned off as necessary for daily laundering, cooking, and cleaning. Chickens scratched the soil and pecked at herbs planted in a kitchen garden that was an inevitable part of the era.

Today, muddied carriages no longer rumble through the massive doors, and the carriageway has become a subdued, welcoming entry that sets a mood of peaceful quiet. The expansive courtyard embodies the style, ambience, and *tout ensemble* of gardens that were created when the Vieux Carré was young: gardens that focused on the romantic, sensuous nature of Creoles, the sons, daughters, and latter-day descendants of colonial Louisiana's French and Spanish settlers.

The bricked court, viewed from the far end of the space, provides a sitting area where guests may take their PETIT DÉJEUNER in the mornings, tea in the afternoon, or just sit quietly during their stay in the Vieux Carré.

This 1860s Belgian stove of nickel-plated iron is tiled in yellow and blue patterns. The stove is used as a planter for prolific Swedish ivy and a base for the potted COLUMNEA, or goldfish plant, which drapes its fascinating cascade of brilliant slender blooms over the ivy, to spill down the stove's front and sides. A side fountain and small pond add the necessary sounds of trickling water to the court.

Next to the pond is a dense growth of palmetto, pink impatiens, and the oldest tree in the court-yard, a sweet olive tree — OSMANTHUS FRA-GRANS. Nearby, a butterfly ginger flower gives off its sweet gardenia-like fragrance.

From the upper balcony is a view into the court over a bower of magenta bougainvillea . . .

while in a corner below, a younger bougainvillea
stretches its branches out of an old Spanish olive
oil jar. A parting view through another arch gives
a panorama of the entire courtyard.

Suarez

*I*n the early softness of an overcast summer's morning, the approach to this home reveals the elegance of this quadrant of the Vieux Carré. The beauty of the edifices in this environ has been maintained by meticulous restoration. This lovely house has a secret garden kept in a pure and authentic manner true to its original design.

The 1832 structure was designed and built by a group of New Orleans architects for an owner who intended to lease it. Abraham Suarez, owner of the newly completed structure, placed an advertisement in the *Courier,* an early New Orleans newspaper, on September 1, 1832, which read as follows:

> *TO LEASE*
>
> A two story brick house, situated in Hospital Street between Royal and Bourbon, newly built by the Architects Company, calculated for a genteel family; has good back buildings, and possession will be given on the first day of November next. For terms apply to A. A. SUAREZ OR GORDON, FORSTALL & COMPANY.

Hospital Street was so named for the location of the military hospital down a short way toward the river from this address on what is now Governor Nicholls Street. The street's present appellation comes from an early Louisiana governor. General Francis T. Nicholls, who had already distinguished himself for his bravery in the Civil War, was elected in 1876 as the Louisiana Democratic candidate chosen to redeem the power of the state from the radical carpetbagger regime then in control. Nicholls served as governor from 1877 to 1880 and from 1888 to 1892. Governor Nicholls Street is the location of numerous splendid homes and gardens.

The welcoming yellow color of the building's facade, with its deep green shutters, draws us to the building itself. The entrance at the left of the facade opens to a corridor, leading back to the courtyard, slave quarters, and stair leading to the upper living quarters of the front and back building. The coolness of the corridor is striking in contrast to the heat of the street. It causes condensation, which glazes the old slates of the walk with a sheen of reflected light.

A pot of yellow cymbidium orchids, with their long graceful leaves, reflects the building's exterior colors and brightens the open arch into the courtyard. The court is sparse, yet each nook is artistically arranged.

Along the wall there is a cluster of decorative pots containing variegated English ivy, plumbago, and sorrel, flanking a space for comfortable alfresco dining. The face of a garden nymph peeks out from the rim of the larger of the vessels; a contented smile is composed on the face.

The large tub hanging on the wall was once used for the washing of kitchenware and the blueing of fine white linens and clothing.

The corner bed, where a well or cistern once existed, now makes a home for an early spring growth of bananas and caladiums.

The soap caldron, once present in every courtyard in New Orleans, now stands suspended as a bed for plumbago.

An alcove in the far end of the back building houses a potting area, where a table and garden tools are kept. A large asparagus fern rests on the table, and an antique copper watering can sits on the flagged surface of the ground below.

The stones used in surfacing the ground in this courtyard are some of the original ballast stones once carried from France and Spain to weight the empty ships, which would be loaded with sugar, cotton, and indigo on their return.

A unique fireplace grate with a lady's face in the center, fired of terra-cotta, is an elegant piece of artistry.

Serene and quiet, this secret garden is an escape from the outside, a place to sit and enjoy being unnoticed as the bustle of the street passes by.

A wooden bench serves as a quiet place for a respite from the day's chores or for a relaxing conversation in the cool of the garden with a visiting friend. A papyrus plant sits beside the bench. Two folding French bistro chairs provide space for more visitors.

Tennessee

New Orleans in general, and the French Quarter in particular, have been inspirational to generations of novelists and poets; titles of all genres continue to keep the city's literary tradition alive. Through the years, writers have been drawn to the city, spending time to write their poetry, stories, and novels about New Orleans. It has always been a romantic and economical city for writers to reside in, two elements necessary to most writers for periods of their careers. Most of the writers who are linked through their work to the Crescent City were not born here; many have journeyed here to develop their work.

Mark Twain and George Washington Cable were friends when they were here at the same time. Edna Ferber placed a scene from her *Saratoga Trunk* in the upstairs dining room of a restaurant in the Vieux Carré. Lafcadio Hearn came here as an educated vagabond and became a well-respected newspaper columnist. Lyle Saxon encouraged William Faulkner to live in New Orleans, persuading him to begin writing novels as well as poetry. Faulkner's *Soldier's Pay* was written in a building on Pirate's Alley, which now houses the Faulkner Book Store. And there was Frances Parkinson Keyes, who wrote the famous *Dinner at Antoine's,* and Sherwood Anderson. Kate Chopin, the author of *The Awakening,* moved to New Orleans shortly after her marriage in 1870.

New Orleans is a city that cannot be denied its literary history. More recent authors, such as Truman Capote, have claimed New Orleans as their home, and Anne Rice, who was born here, has recently returned to reside permanently.

If, however, there is a single author who has tied himself to this city through his work, it is Tennessee Williams. Williams's play *A Streetcar Named Desire* is one of the most indelible pieces ever to have been created for, and seemingly dedicated to, a city. The title came from an actual streetcar line that ran down Desire Street.

For Williams, New Orleans was the place where he could retreat into his personal melancholy, a condition he said resulted from the "foxbite of loneliness." It was in New Orleans that the children of his heart came alive.

In his later years, Tennessee Williams owned a home in the Vieux Carré where he lived during his many visits. He installed a pool in the deep court and spent happier times here.

Preceding page:

The rear court has a kidney-shaped pool that was installed by Tennessee. Old bricks have been attractively arranged in patterns to accentuate the shape of the pool. Large palms grow in the corners of the court. The back wall is planted with a bed of pink impatiens, while tall slender tree branches offer additional privacy to the area.

The building and side court are typical Vieux Carré buildings. The flagged surfacing has irregularly sized stones, ballast from empty ships coming to collect trade cargo in the colony, and a large sugar caldron as a planter. Loquat, bamboo, cedar, and Japanese yew surround the court. Hanging baskets of Boston fern help to fill the open space between the building and the trees.

New Guinea impatiens, with lovely orange flowers and shiny dark leaves, are scattered about in the beds in contrast to the pink impatiens.

A potted magenta bougainvillea stands aside a gate entering a side yard. The wisteria in this area gives a magnificent display of its draping lavender flowers. These clusters of buds are falling to the ground, painting the brick surface with a coat of lavender.

A small back fountain contains a richly purple iris resembling velvet. Other planters contain varieties of tulips, some yellow and red, others purely red.

A turtle, who lives in this garden, languishes in the bed of wisteria petals, waiting for his next meal to appear.

Tropical

Over the course of the history of New Orleans, as it was passed in ownership and rule from the French to the Spanish, back to the French, and then to the United States, several major conflagrations virtually destroyed most of its original buildings. It is because of this that much of the architectural charm of the French Quarter is actually of Spanish design. Even the French Market is a Spanish building, though the market at that location existed from the founding of the city in 1718 as an Indian trading post.

All of the private residence buildings in the Vieux Carré replace prior dwellings that were destroyed, or torn down, and rebuilt in the architectural style of the day. This small residence, built in 1831, was restored in the 1970s. The deep and narrow courtyard with its lovely garden is an excellent example of how well a narrow space can be horticulturally designed. This is also an excellent example of the exquisite tropical foliage and flora that can grow in a New Orleans garden.

The peach-and-turquoise color scheme of the structure opens up the space, allowing it to breathe, giving the court the illusion of a much greater space. The Caribbean feeling of these colors is magnified by the choice of equatorial verdure.

The entire bordering wall to the left of the entry-way has at its base an elongated planter bed that extends to the very rear of the property. The leaves of the bananas lean heavily over and into the walk, upholding a purple heartlike bloom into the sky overhead. These treelike perennials gained popularity in New Orleans during the 1840s and have ever since been an indispensable component of the city's foliage.

Lush leaves of a ginger reach out over the path, as do the bananas, pulling in the sun that slides down into the narrow path. A window box of pink geraniums and dusty miller help break the continuous color flow of the building.

An unexpected bonsai contrasts nicely, not only
with the other foliage but also with the backdrop
of the partially closed batten shutters.

The back corner of the court is a cascade of greenery. Thick masses of wisteria climb high, while
caladiums hug the ground around the fountain.

Orange-red trumpet flowers, CAMPSIS RADICANS, *suspend behind leaves of a ginger, with a holly fern behind.*

A small cockspur coral tree, ERYTHRINA CRISTA-GALLI, *with some of its blooms unfolding, is accompanied underneath by both white and pink caladiums. The scarlet open blooms of the cockspur coral tree are stunning in their exotic beauty.*

The corner of the wall adjoining the building houses a rustic wooden bird shelter and feeder. The shadowed silhouette of leaves dappled against the shutters asserts the tropical feel of this secret garden.

Photograph Acknowledgments

Transparencies for the pages listed here were taken by
Glade Bilby II. All others were taken by the author,
Roy F. Guste, Jr.

Arsenal: 14, 16
Begue: 32 (top and bottom), 34
Bijou: 38, 43 (right), 47
Conflagration: 78, 80, 87
Heguy: 88, 91, 92, 93
Jalousie: 108 (right), 109, 110, 111
Patti: 139, 140 (right), 141, 142
Soniat: 168, 171, 175, 177
Suarez: 181, 182
Tennessee: 188, 190 (top), 191, 192 (bottom), 193